Life after the Change:
Receiving What God Has for You

LIFE AFTER THE CHANGE

Tiffany Robinson

Copyright

© 2018 Tiffany Robinson. All rights reserved.

ISBN-13: 978-0692195420 (Too Real, LLC)

ISBN-10: 0692195424

No part of this book may be reproduced or transmitted in any form or by any means, electronic or mechanical, including photocopying, recording or by any information storage and retrieval system, without written permission from the author, except for the inclusion of brief quotations in a review.

Published by: Too Real, LLC, Marietta, GA 30008

Printed in the United States of America

Note: This book is intended to give you hope for your life and how to be at peace while making a change in your life. Readers are advised to reach out for further help, if needed, before making any changes with your life. The information in this book is based on the author's beliefs and experiences in life. The author cannot be held responsible for any actions that may be encountered.

Other titles by Tiffany Robinson

Born to Change

DEDICATION

I knew that you would make it. God has a plan for you. It doesn't matter what they say or what they're doing; this celebration is all for you. That's why this book is dedicated to you.

CONTENTS

Life after the Change

You Gotta Go through it to Get to It

Don't Limit Yourself

Your Future is Calling

Follow the Leader

Winning

Be Thankful

Stay Humble

You're Not Alone

You Got This!

Life after the Change

"You can't stop your birth, and you can't stop your death, but you sure can live your best life…no excuses!"

~ Tiffany Robinson

Whew! Now, who said, "Change is easy"? Not I! But you did it. I did it. We all can do it. You made it. I made it. We all can. Well, first, I am here to celebrate with you. You did all the steps outlined in my first book, *Born to Change*. You changed your surroundings. You started loving yourself. You started putting God first. You started forgiving others. You started forgiving yourself. You did everything you needed to in order to change, so good for you. Now, I didn't say it was going to be easy to get here. I only shared the steps that I took to get myself here, but I want you to know that I am still taking this journey with you. I am right here with you, and I will be with you every step of the way. I am no different than you. I'm living this, too. I'm just who God created me to be, and so are you! You already know you were *Born to Change*, so don't you think it is time to explore what life is like *after the change*?

***

The title *Life after the Change* holds a lot of significance for me. The phrase *life after the change* acknowledges that there has been a shift, a turnaround. It means that something has happened – you've changed. It means you have set a goal and accomplished it. It means you were able to make your way through a difficult time and come out on the other side. Congratulations! You deserve to celebrate. You deserve to feel proud of your accomplishments. You've done what a lot of people wish they could do but have never done – you changed.

I know you must be wondering, What do I do now? What can I expect from *life after the change*?

You most definitely can expect to see the outcome of the changes you have already made while working toward your next goal. Without a doubt, you are a work in progress. If you think of yourself as such, you will always be open to doing the work that needs to get done to help you live a more fulfilled life. We'll get into this a little later, but first, we need to celebrate!

***

From the moment you were conceived, you have been in a constant state of change. You have been consistently growing. When you were in your mother's belly, your growth was an important indicator of your health and development. If, every time she went to a doctor's appointment, there was no growth and further development, that would be an indication that something was wrong, but as you continued to grow and develop, the date of your arrival continued to approach, and once you had completed your nine months' journey inside your mother's womb, you were ready to make the first big change of your life – being born.

Whether your birth took thirty minutes or thirty hours, you came into this world, kicking and screaming and, without even knowing it, changing. Your birth definitely changed and impacted many lives. You became an important and much-loved member of a family and a community. You were doted on and cared for by many people, including family and friends. Your very existence changed their lives.

From birth, because you were unaware of how hard it would be later in life, you changed and adapted constantly. You probably went from sleeping during the day to sleeping at night, just a few weeks after you were born. You probably went from being breastfed to eating whole foods within a few months. You probably went from crawling to walking by the time you were one. You probably went from wearing diapers and having to be changed ten times a day to being completely potty trained by the time you were two. Lastly, you probably went from being unable to speak to talking people's heads off by the time you were ready for kindergarten. Think of all the changing you did within the first five years of your life. Think of how you changed without even knowing you were doing so because you were growing up.

Now, think about where you are in your life right now. You've changed. I would like for you to now think about this: What other changes do you need to make to continue to grow? Is it difficult to think about these other changes because you've lost your ability to adapt and grow without putting too much thought into it like you did when you were a child? Why is that? What is stopping you?

As stated at the beginning of this chapter, you must applaud, congratulate, and celebrate yourself when you accomplish something, but you must not stop at one change because there will always be more to improve. For example, just because you have lost twenty pounds doesn't mean you now have perfect credit. Part of living this life means that we are able to elevate many things to many levels; sometimes, we make these elevations simultaneously, and sometimes, we elevate only one thing at a time. Your change may be something as drastic as ending a life-threatening drug habit or something as non-life-threatening as ending your annoying nail-biting habit, but ending both of these habits indicates your ability to exert control over your life, so being able to change, no matter how big or small, is significant.

***

So here you are, starting fresh. Did you celebrate yourself for doing so? You don't have to throw yourself a huge party, but, did you, at least, pat yourself on the back and say, "Hey! Good job, me"? If so, good for you. You have to celebrate your accomplishments. If you haven't, why not? But don't worry. I am here to celebrate with you. I want you to be proud of yourself. I want you to realize how happy God is for you just for making the changes you have already made, and I want you to know that you can change even more and accomplish even more of your goals. Celebrate yourself. Do your happy dance. You know you deserve it.

***

I just want to applaud you for changing because that's just what *Life after the Change* is – a celebration. By the end of this book, I want you to understand that change is always going to occur because it is a necessity. It is a part of your journey and a part of our experience as humans. Simply put, *Life after the Change* means that there will always be more to look forward to.

You Gotta Go through it to Get to It

"You can listen to a million people, but if you don't listen to God, you ain't heard nothing."

~ Tiffany Robinson

I want to congratulate you for realizing that the only way to make your life better is to change. If you had just stayed where you were, would your life have improved on its own? I doubt it, so I am proud of you for making it happen. I would like to encourage you to continue to do what is necessary to improve your life.

I am sure there were times, especially when you were in the middle of bettering yourself, when it got really, really rough, and when it did, I am sure all you wanted to do was quit. Again, I am so, so glad you didn't. You realized that *you gotta go through it to get to it*. Change is what I want you to focus on because it is something that you never stop doing, no matter what. This is something that we have to do daily.

Life after the Change focuses on staying in the change because, once we change, what happens? Sometimes, our old ways try to come back, so if we don't make the decision to continue to improve ourselves, there will be a heavier chance that we will be pulled back into our old ways, so be careful. Changing doesn't mean everything is set in stone. It's not saying, "Hey! I'm free. I don't do that, and I don't do this" because, when the trying times come, you have to make sure you have the strength to win over your past ways.

You've got to know that the devil is always trying to set you up. The devil wants you to fail. Once you change, it's very easy for what you thought was your past to sneak back in just to test your strength. You will be tested more. You will be challenged more. Once you've realized that you've changed, you will be like the Energizer bunny. You'll keep going and going and going. Nothing stays the same. I am sure you know that nothing ever stays the same because changing is a part of your journey, but don't worry, as you navigate, you will notice trusting God with your path will bring forth your vision. A lot of your changes, also known as hopes, dreams, and goals, will make sense and will fall into place.

***

How do you go through it to get to it? Think about what it's like on your way to work. Not very many of us get to say, "I love my commute to work," unless you work from home. Other than that, every morning, you have to get up super early. Then, you have to take a shower and brush your teeth. After showering, you get dressed. Next, you eat breakfast or just grab a quick cup of coffee. With your travel mug in your hand, you hop in your car, and, after pulling out of your driveway, you get on the road. When you think about the hour-long drive and the bumper-to-bumper traffic you have to be in, it might make you want to call in, but you realize that you have to go through all that traffic to get to your destination. If you don't, then you probably won't get paid, and you would probably lose your job. Now the question is, how can you make going through it to get to it work to your advantage?

One thing you can do is remember what it felt like when you applied for the job and prayed for that phone call/email that would make a difference. How did you feel? I am sure you felt hopeful. Maybe making your commute more enjoyable requires your attitude about driving to work to shift a little. We have to force ourselves to see the brighter side of things because, sometimes, we have to make ourselves do things we don't want to, so in order to "get through them," it is best that we adjust our approach to them. It's really all about perspective, so if we really think going to work is the worst thing ever, think about the people who don't have jobs who desperately need one. Think about the people who don't have a car or access to public transportation who desperately need it, so, if you don't like driving to work, why not transform your experience? Listen to an audiobook to educate or entertain yourself as you prepare for your next level. Listen to your favorite music and sing along at the top of your lungs while the wind blows through your hair. You can turn difficult things into positive, learning experiences. You have the power to do anything and everything you want to do.

***

Often, right when you're about to have a breakthrough, the "going through it" becomes extremely difficult. A good example of this is when you're losing weight and you're almost at your goal. Many people believe the last five pounds are the hardest to lose, so if you go a week without losing those five pounds, but you're still working out hard and eating right, you might feel like all hope is lost. I am here to tell you that you have to keep working. You can't stop because, if you don't do anything, if you give up because of one little setback, you definitely won't lose the weight or achieve whatever your goal is. Remember, it's always right before you reach your goal that you are hit with seemingly insurmountable obstacles and setbacks, but you have to keep going. *You gotta go through it to get to it!* Let me repeat that. *You gotta go through it to get to it!* You have to go through that difficult time, just like when Jesus was being tempted while he fasted for forty days (Matthew 4:1-11). Not having food for all that time was hard enough, but then the devil was there to tempt him. Jesus wasn't necessarily changing, but through fasting, he showed how important sacrifice is. The devil thought Jesus would be very vulnerable and easy to manipulate because he hadn't had food, but he wasn't. He remained mentally strong the whole time. God is not going to forsake you during your challenges, especially when you are at your most difficult stages of growth.

You have been blessed with discernment, so use it. It's there for a reason, so *you gotta go through it to get to it*. No matter what you're changing, don't allow the devil to make you think you were or are wrong for changing, so don't feel bad about improving more things about yourself. Know that getting through the most difficult parts of your journey will make your life that much sweeter and that much more appreciated.

***

There is no such thing as you change, and then you stop. In other words, once you start to escalate, you'll keep escalating because you'll keep finding and looking for more things to improve. You're compelled to do this because we're literally changing every single day of our lives. Nobody ever just changes, and then that's it. As we continue to grow, we realize more about ourselves. You know, we might even stop eating fried foods, even after we said that would never happen (LOL!), so you know change is all around us. We must be products of this and welcome it.

After reading *Born to Change*, you learned that you couldn't hide from the person you were created to be. You might have had some very tough days while you were in the midst of finding yourself. You might have been unsure at times, and that's okay. The important thing is that you kept pushing through. The important thing is that you came out on the other side. Unknowingly, you taught yourself a very powerful lesson. You learned that you have the ability to persevere and stay strong, even when you probably felt like giving up, but look at you now. Look at what you have accomplished. As I said in the first chapter, you have every right and reason to celebrate. Laugh, dance, and sing in celebration of your accomplishments. Do this for as long as you want to because I want you to take this positivity with you as you enjoy your journey.

***

One analogy that comes to mind is our journey through school. Think about all the *going through it to get to it* you had to do during those first twelve years of your education. First, there was kindergarten. Can you remember what your first day of school was like? Were you scared? Were you excited? Did you cry when you realized that your parents couldn't stay with you? Were you happy about making new friends? Think about that first day and what you had to do to get through it. Now, think about all the ups and downs you had during your first year. This was probably one of the times when you learned the most. What you learned during this first year helped to lay the foundation for the rest of your academic career. Most of us didn't walk in knowing our alphabet and numbers. Instead, each and every day, we learned a little bit more and a little bit more until, by the end of the year, we were able to say our ABCs and count from one to one hundred. Then, we celebrated the completion of kindergarten and prepared for first grade.

Now, in first grade, we were able to build on what we had learned in kindergarten, but when they put that oversized pencil or crayon in our tiny hands, it probably took each of us a few days to get used it, but we did, didn't we? And by the end of the year, we were writing our names and short, simple sentences and drawing pictures of our families. Soon, we celebrated the end of the first grade and prepared for the second grade.

A few years later, we were entering junior high. Along with a new year of learning, we also got to experience puberty. Talk about *going through it to get to it*, but somehow, we made it through. And a few years after that, we reached our senior year in high school.

Now how did you feel about reaching this point? I am sure you felt a mixture of fear and triumph. You probably were fearful because you didn't really know what to expect next. After all that time and hard work, you were at the end of a very long journey. Ultimately, you felt triumphant because you had reached a very important milestone, and what did you do? Most likely, you celebrated, and there was a need for a celebration because you had worked hard and achieved a lot. You had gone through it, and you had gotten to it. Your diploma was proof of that, so you deserved to pat yourself on the back.

I want you to think of changing, just like you did during your high school graduation. Just like school, changing was probably a little scary at times, but you kept with it, and very soon, you were on the road to success, and because you believed in your ability to triumph, you did not quit, not even when it became hard or when seeing the light at the end of the tunnel became difficult. You kept with it, making your way through the darkness until you saw the light. And that is why you *must* celebrate.

After experiencing the success of changing, you should be on a high. You know what it feels like to set your mind on something and accomplish it. Yes, you rocked it!

Now that you know what it takes to set and achieve your goals, you will be better prepared for all the other goals you are about to conquer. I think it is important for you to think back to how you got through those times. You must remember how you were able to power through. Prepare yourself to call on that same fortitude because, nine times out of ten, you *will* call on it, especially now that you have some experience with what comes with change, and you know how important it is. As you embark on your next level, know that you will encounter more resistance, but you must also know that it will truly be worth it.

***

Going through it can range from a small, insignificant setback to a major catastrophe. No matter how big or small it is, what matters most is your attitude toward it and your ability to not let it hold you back from reaching your goals.

For example, sometimes, when we are ready to change, the hardest thing to do is to get started. When you want to begin a diet, why does it seem like, on the very day you decide to start, one of your coworkers comes to work with one dozen of your favorite donuts? The answer, I am sure you know, is clear. This is your first little test. This test determines how serious you are about making a difference. So, while the aroma of those warm, glaze-covered donuts fills the room, you must decide if starting your diet today is more important than one last indulgence.

Another example could be that you've decided to start saving money. On the day that you decide to move some money into a separate savings account, you get hit with a large, urgent bill that must be paid immediately. Now, you probably don't have any choice but to pay this bill, but you must also remember that you cannot let this bill ruin your plans. You are just getting started, so you cannot let this stop you from changing your plan to save more money. It is a minor setback, not a permanent defeat.

Once you have started making a difference, you would like to think that it will be smooth sailing, but I am sure you know that this is generally not the case. You know that you will most likely encounter very rough waves on your way to completing your goal. This is what happens when you're halfway there, and I believe it happens because you *are* halfway there. Your commitment to change gets tested.

To use the weight loss example again, say you are halfway to your weight loss goal when you realize that you haven't lost any weight in two weeks. And you probably don't understand why since you've been working out harder and eating more salads and drinking a gallon of water every day.

When you realize this, you might get a little sad because you don't know what you are doing wrong. While you are in this bad place, you remember that there is still chocolate cake in your fridge from a party you attended. Because you are upset about the lack of progress, you think seriously about eating that whole cake because your mind is telling you, "What difference will it make?"

This is a simple example, but it is significant. While you are changing, especially when you are in process of it, you must understand that you will not always see or feel it while it is happening. In the beginning, you may have experienced rapid and very clear differences in whatever your area of change is, but after that initial flurry of excitement, the dust will settle, and the change will become a little routine, and it won't feel brand new anymore because now it is a part of your life. This is when your obstacles will show up, so be prepared. Don't get discouraged. Also, be kind to yourself. So, if you are tempted to eat that chocolate cake, what will you do? You have many choices. Depending on how strict your diet is, you could eat a tiny slice. And if you do eat it, enjoy it and move on. Don't beat yourself up. Just get past that craving and then get back into *going through it* mode. This is the only way you can *get through it*. You must be someone who can live in the present and be forward-thinking. Know that a challenge is coming and prepare yourself for that challenge as much as you possibly can. When you prepare, you can almost always guarantee that you will be successful.

Now imagine you're at the end of your plan. Let's say you're two pounds away from reaching your weight goal. It's so close, yet so far away. Just as it was when you started, the end can present its own set of difficulties. Be prepared for this, so you can *get through it*. Know that you have worked so hard and accomplished so much. This isn't even a hurdle; it's a tiny, little pebble that you merely have to step over. Keep your perspective about this, and you will always, always, always be successful.

***

Chinese philosopher Lao Tzu stated, "A journey of a thousand miles begins with a single step." Your job on the road to self-improvement in this life is to take that first step. As long as you are putting one foot in front of the other and moving forward, no one can fault you for how quickly or how slowly you change. You are the determining factor in your progress. You are the one who decides how you approach your change and at what speed you get it done.

It is important to remember that, when it gets tough, all you have to do is keep moving forward, keep putting one foot in front of the other. This is how you *get through it.* This is how you make progress. If you keep your goal in mind, regardless of your outside circumstances, you will prevail, just like you already have and just like you will continue to do.

If you feel like you are being tested and if you feel like you are about to give up, think about Jesus and his forty-day fast while being tempted by the devil. Think about what it must have felt like to deprive his body of food for that long. Then, think about what it must have been like to be tempted by the devil when he was at his most vulnerable and at his weakest. Think about how much inner strength he had to have had to not fall for the devil's game. You have that same strength within in you. Did you know that?

It is something that you use every day. It is something that you tap into at will.

Remember *you gotta go through it to get to it*, and you deserve only the best of everything, especially when you devote yourself to improving your life and work hard for it.

Don't Limit Yourself

"Don't be surprised, just be prepared."

~ Tiffany Robinson

I think this advice is so important that I had to name one of my chapters – Don't Limit Yourself. The first thing I think you should know is that you should always reach and want for more. We all have hopes and dreams, but sometimes, those hopes and dreams are limited by the way we think. Remember, we should never limit our visions; they are a part of our hopes, our dreams, and our goals. We should know and acknowledge that, sometimes, we see our lives through tunnel vision, and, sometimes, we don't believe in ourselves enough to make it happen. We do have the potential to live our dreams.

If the part of your life that you want to improve involves making more money, let me give you a quick example. What would you do if your goal was to make $50,000 a year, which is about $1,000 per week? Now imagine you landed a job that paid you exactly that amount. After you have been on that job for two weeks, what would you do if someone offered you a job making double that amount? Would you turn down the offer because you had reached your desired goal? Or would you take up the new offer? This might seem very simplistic, but it happens a lot. Often, we settle for where we are because it's better than where we've been. Why? I believe it is because we fear our own potential to be great. I believe it is because we are afraid of setting a goal to change and actually achieving that goal. I believe that some of us don't believe we deserve to live absolutely amazing lives.

There was a time when I was truly struggling. I wasn't happy with my living situation, but even then, I knew that, one day, I would be a homeowner, so I went from being homeless, to living with others, to living in an apartment, to moving into a townhome. I never lost sight of my vision of owning my own home. Yes, I could have lived in a townhome because it was better than what I was used to; however, God always wants more for you, so why not do whatever it takes for your vision to come to the light? I did, and so should you.

So now is the time to ask yourself, what changes have you tried to make that have not gone well because you limited the potential outcome? Even better, what changes have you tried to make where you achieved those changes too easily because your goals were too easy, too attainable, or not challenging enough?

Think about some of the people you admire. And think about how they did not limit themselves. Think about Michael Jordan and how he was eliminated from the basketball team in high school. He could have let that end his career. Instead, he began training with even more passion and determination, and we all know what he achieved. Think about Oprah Winfrey, and how she was fired from her first job. She did not let that stop her from ruling daytime TV for twenty-five years, and now she owns her own network. Now think about yourself. Even though changing is a revolutionary act, are you being revolutionary enough? Where are you limiting your growth? Are you settling?

You've already shown that you have the ability to conquer what it takes to change. Now it's time to dream bigger and bolder for yourself. What do you want? What do you really want?

It is very important to evaluate each and every change that you plan to make and to make sure that you are doing something that is achievable but also challenging. You know that you are capable of making a change, and this book is a celebration of that, but you should also stretch yourself while evolving because it should take you out of your comfort zone. It should make you a little bit or a lot uncomfortable, but in the end, you will have achieved something bigger than your vision.

I am sure you have experienced times in your life where you received more than you expected. It gave you a good feeling, didn't it? The idea of receiving more is always a good thing, especially if you were settling. It is important for you to set goals, but it is just as important for you to leave room for those goals to grow and expand beyond what you intended. Doing this allows miracles to happen. Doing this will allow you to see how your efforts can bring forth bigger and better achievements.

As we stated in the last chapter, all you have to do is take the first step, from there, you will be guided to do what you need and have to do to reach your desired goal, so if you get the chance to return to college to get your bachelor's degree, please don't turn down the opportunity to get your master's degree on their new fast-track program, just because it wasn't a part of your original plan. Sometimes, you don't know about the opportunities that are available because they are still being worked out. Changing, sometimes, requires flexibility. If you are hard and rigid, you will snap like a tree, but if you remain fluid and amendable, you'll be able to adapt to any new situation quickly and gracefully, especially since the situation that is placed before you is meant to improve your life.

Don't limit yourself by thinking the life you're living is it. If you don't like your current health status, living situation, or financial situation, you can change it. Once you've committed to change, allow God to take over. Just be ready to receive more than you might have originally expected. He has been waiting for you to take that first bold step, and once you've done that, he may say, "Let's turn that $50,000 into one million dollars!" Are you going to argue with God? I hope not.

Your Future is Calling

"Let your faith be your inspiration. Only you see your vision. Let God be your motivation. He created you."

~ Tiffany Robinson

Because we are celebrating all that we have grown to be, we should wake up every morning full of happiness. Actually, you should jump out of bed every morning, knowing that you have a chance to do better. You should know that you are able to do the necessary work to improve your life. Knowing this, you should know that your future is bright.

Life after the Change has taught me that *you gotta go through it to get to it* and that you shouldn't *limit yourself* because *your future is calling*. Your future may seem far away at times, but in reality, it is only one second away. All you have to do is work more toward your dreams and goals, and you have begun to do just that. Remember, the journey of one-thousand miles begins with one step.

We all know that, sometimes, the hardest thing to do is to find our purpose, but once you've made that decision, you will notice that everything, everybody around you, is different. Yes, I've talked about how hard it can be to change, but I want to make sure you know that difficulties come with their own benefits. It might be difficult, but in the end, there will be a changed you, a new you.

Your future is only what your faith is. Your life will grow only if you believe you are worthy of more. This belief is based on your faith. Do you believe you deserve more? If you do or even if you don't, know that God has already created a provision for your life. I am sure you've asked God to give you the strength to prepare you for more, and since you are reading this book, I know that you have noticed that God has done just that. In order to stay in the change, you need two things – you need to have faith in your future, and you need to believe in your faith. With these two things, you are able to make the difference that you've set out to make.

This is, sometimes, easier said than done because I am sure that there have been times when what you wanted to change seemed very daunting and unchangeable. Maybe you wanted to get out of a bad living situation or stop a habit that was threatening your health and well-being. Remember, all you need is faith the size of a mustard seed (Matthew 17:20). Along with believing in it, you will see the provision that God has for your life; your belief will unfold. You just need to have (a little) faith.

Don't give up. You've got to know that your faith will carry you through to your future. You will get to where you need to go but only if you don't give up. Once you have started on your next level, you have to keep leveling up. If you wanted it bad enough to start, please know you have more than enough faith to finish it.

By believing in your faith, your future is waiting on you, and you will also notice that your bad days turn out to be your better days, and you will be positively impacting your life and possibly even the lives of those around you.

Know that you will be able to change and get out of your comfort zone by the grace of God. God will give you the strength to push yourself out of your boundaries, whether it be off the couch or into a better living situation.

Now that you have your faith firmly in place, you have to know that giving up is not an option. Once you have decided to trust God with your journey, you are now guaranteed to grow. You cannot stop in the middle of it, especially if you are doing something that will drastically improve your life. You've got to know that, sometimes, you won't just go from living out of your car to living in a mansion. Sometimes, you will go from being homeless, to living with relatives, to an apartment, to a townhome, then to owning your home. This has been my personal journey, and what I've learned is, if you don't give up on yourself, you will see your desired outcome.

Every day, we get to decide what our future will look like. If we stay prayed up and if we stay faithful, our futures will always look bright. God will always be there. He will always and continually give us the strength and courage we need to make it through. He did not put us on this earth to just stay in one place. He did not put us on this earth to live in turmoil. Yes, sometimes, we are put in difficult situations, so we can see that we have the ability to grow and improve. Sometimes, we have to be a little uncomfortable because that discomfort is what we need to prompt us to live our best lives.

***

Now that you've changed and know that your future is calling, you must be wondering, What does the future hold? This whole book is dedicated to that. In order to celebrate your bright future, there are two things that you must be willing to do, and that is keep putting God first and keep changing.

What can you do now to continue evolving? My first suggestion is to write down what you changed and how you feel about it. Write openly and honestly about your feelings. Some questions to answer could be: What was the change? When did I start it? When did I complete it? Did I feel forced to change? Was I happy about making this change? Did this change improve my life for the better? If so, do I see how this change improved my life? If not, was this change meant to improve my life? What areas of my life were affected by this change? Did this change improve my relationship with myself and others?

After you have answered these questions or others that you have created, put them in a place where you can reread them often, especially if you feel yourself getting sad about or becoming unsatisfied with the outcome.

Now, after you've written about the change you've made, use that same notebook to write about other changes you'd like to make. Take an assessment of every area of your life – health, religion/spirituality, love/relationships, family, work/career/education, finances, travel, and goals. You can assess all of these or just the one that applies. Just as before, you must be open and honest about your feelings in each category.

For instance, using health as an example again, start by asking yourself, how is my health? From there, write down if your health is where you want it to be. If it's not, what will you have to do to change it? Has it been a while since you've been to the doctor? Do you need to start exercising regularly? Do you get enough sleep? Will taking a daily multi-vitamin improve your health?

Ask yourself deep, searching questions for each category. After answering the questions, you can then begin to work on your hopes, dreams, and goals. It won't be easy, but it will be worth it, especially if you ask God for help.

Having God by your side is so important. I really wouldn't even recommend that you try to change without asking God for guidance. As you change, prayer is a tool that you can use to directly connect with God and ask for help when you feel yourself becoming discouraged. You do not have to do this alone. God will guide your every step. Your relationship with God will give you the peace you need to make the right choices.

The most important thing you need to always remember is that God did not bring you this far just to leave you. In this life, you have a constant companion. You just have to realize that you are so loved. That changing for the better is a wonderfully beautiful thing in God's eyes. God has given you the will and the determination to do whatever you need. Remember this whenever you feel overwhelmed.

Know that developing a relationship with God will only benefit you. Your relationship with God will give you strength, courage, and determination. Believe me because I know from personal experience. You can do anything you set your mind to when you have God on your side.

***

Your future is calling. Your future is only what your faith is. Decide to put your faith and trust in God. Stay prayed up and prayerful and just see what amazing changes will come into your life. Know that, as a child of God, all that he wants is for you to live a blessed and prosperous life. The struggles, setbacks, and difficulties are not meant to be permanent. They are meant to be temporary, and they are meant to only teach a lesson, which is the blessing. They are not meant to define you or be who or what you are for the rest of your life. Remember, your future is calling, and your future is only what your faith is.

Follow the Leader

"When you walk by faith and not by sight, you will see how blind others are to your vision. That's why God created it just for you."

~ Tiffany Robinson

In *Born to Change*, I stressed the importance of maintaining a relationship with God because, if you don't believe in a higher power, which is Jesus Christ, the son of God, change isn't understandable. God's lead is the best to follow on your journey.

After improving our lives for the better, some people think, Well, man, I changed today, so I'm good. I want to tell those people, "Do you know what I went through just to get to *life after the change*? Do you know what I went through to make my changes happen? Do you know about the sacrifices I had to make for myself and my family? Are you willing to make continuous sacrifices? Because that is what I am doing and have done, and I am no different than you. We are all the same." I just want to say, "Yes, I've been there."

I gave the power to God, and I want to encourage you to give God the power. Please don't give your power to people. That's not what God wants.

So often, after coaching/counseling those in need of my services, they will say, "Tiffany Robinson made me go to God." Why? Because I am simply a conduit for him. It's my job to lead people to him. I'll help you, but I will always tell you that you need to go to the source. I am not the source. I'm just the middle man (LOL!), and we are all works in progress. Once you put your faith and trust in God, your future will unfold before you, and you will know that it is meant only and especially for you. Once you listen to and obey God, be ready for the celebration. Yes, changing can be difficult, but once you reach the end of your goal, you will see that change is never-ending. God, who has been there every step of the way, will be there to reward you for being obedient and for trusting what he put in your heart to do.

That's why I say, "Go to the source and not your peers." Your peers are only going to tell you what worked for them or what they have experienced, what they wanted to happen, or what they wished could have or would have happened, so it's very important that you don't ever give up hope.

Everyone has their own unique challenges that they are dealing with. That's why it is difficult to rely on people's advice when you are trying to evolve because we are all dealing with our own difficulties, and we can only see through the lenses of our own perspectives. Someone might have an issue with getting to work, but someone else might have an issue with drugs. Another person might have an issue with one or more of their family members, while someone else might have an issue with finding stable housing. All these issues are very important and might seem daunting and insurmountable to the people dealing with them. These situations might seem impossible to change, but please know that, no matter what you are dealing with, God has already solved them. Instead of asking your fellow man for help, my advice is to go straight to God.

***

Here is a scenario. Have you ever said, "Well, my friend told me that the best thing for me to do is to do this, but then my other friend said that maybe I should do the opposite, and my mom said, 'How about this third option?'" The problem is you should never put people before God. Instead, you should remind yourself to keep God first. Tell yourself, "Hey! God did give us discernment. I will be doing what he has led me to do, no matter what everybody else says." Why? Because God is truly the only being who knows what's best for you. God knows everything about you. He knows your heart, and he knows your past, present, and future. He's the one who blessed you with the strength and the ability to change.

There are a lot of people that don't change because they are incapable of thinking for themselves, let alone having faith in God.

They allow their peers to make decisions for them. Before they change, they take a poll. They basically live their lives the way other people want them to, and that is not what they or we were put on this earth for. To me, that's a form of not having enough confidence within yourself and not having faith in God that everything is going to be okay. The phrase *life after the change* tells me that I did change, no matter what. So, whether you've read my first book, *Born to Change*, or not, if you're reading this book, you have already made changes. In my first book, like I mentioned earlier, I stressed the importance of listening to God and developing a relationship with him. Without him, you are walking through the world deaf and blind. With him, you hear what others can't hear, and you see what other can't see. He already has it all planned out for you; he is just waiting on you. If it worked for you once, why wouldn't it work for you again?

Like I stated in *Born to Change* and in the first chapter of this book, there are several things that you must do in order to change. You must change your surroundings. You must love yourself. You must strengthen your relationship with God. I want to encourage you to push further because, at this point, I am assuming that this is what you want, so don't allow the devil to steal all that away from you.

***

My mom loves to tell the story of how she realized that God had placed a calling on my life when I was three years old. I always waited until I saw that she was busy to ask if I could do this and if I could do that. Sometimes, she would ignore me, and sometimes, she would say yes. One day, I asked her to do something, and she said "yes." Instead of being elated by this, I turned to her and said, "You must not love me if you're going to let me do whatever I want." These words astonished my mom, and she realized that I knew how important having leadership and discipline in my life was. From a very young age, I knew that I needed to follow someone's example in order for my life to go in the right direction. Because I was a very precocious child, I knew I needed guidance, so I wasn't afraid to speak on it when I felt I wasn't getting any or enough, and that is pretty much how my life has been ordered. I follow God's lead because he hasn't ever led me wrong.

***

Because of the challenges I've been through, I want to be here to hold your hand and walk with you on your journey. I want to remind you that you are the solution. It might even be a little painful, but if you know you've been called by God, why not listen to God? I've done it, so should you. You're not alone. I'm doing what I have to do with what God wants me to do. At the end of the day, if you listen to God and follow his lead, you're going to make it.

Just like you, I'm building myself, and it takes a lot to do that. Sometimes, you have to do stuff you don't want to do in order to get things done. I'm not trying to scare you away from your future; I'm trying to encourage you to keep reaching for the stars. You're already not the same person that you used to be because you've made the necessary changes, so I've written this book to encourage you to keep going. Why?

Because the devil doesn't want to see you prosper. The devil wants you to stay in bondage. The devil wants you to live in fear. Just like a hater, that's his whole trick. If the devil can get us to stay the same, to never change, to never get rid of bad, unhealthy, deadly habits, then our lives will never flourish, and we will never call on God for his help, strength, and guidance. When you change, guess what? You defeat the devil, but you, also, have to prepare yourself for a new devil because you're on a new level. Your battle is not going to be the same as it was before. You probably didn't really see anything that you were battling because you were all in it, so when you change, that's when the devil taunts you the most. Think back to Jesus when he was fasting. As the devil tempts you, he might say, "You need to go back to your old ways. Weren't you comfortable then? Why are you stepping out of your comfort zone?" When you are in the midst of growth, what do you think is saving you and keeping you? It's the grace of God. Turn to him for guidance. Let him be your leader.

Winning

"Failure is success, and success is a part of Having faith, so those down days are really preparing you for your up days."

~ Tiffany Robinson

Don't you know that you are winning? Have you been celebrating? Have you been praising God for helping you on your journey? Have you thanked him for bringing you through everything, for turning your bad into your good?

The people who know me are shocked at how happy I am. Why? Because I've been through a lot. Here are a few highlights. My parents divorced when I was thirteen. I was a teenage mother, and I had to deal with an unstable living situation for several years. But none of these obstacles ever made me feel like a loser or that I was losing at life; instead, all these things forced me to win. By the grace of God, I turned my mess into a message, and I know you are doing the same thing. That's why we are celebrating.

***

As I stated earlier, my parents divorced when I was thirteen years old. Their split devasted me. For the first twelve years of my life, I thought I was living the dream. I knew I was loved. I, also, was a very spoiled little girl, so while their divorce was devasting, there were some good things that came out of it. I could have continued down that road of being a very spoiled child, but the dissolution of my parents' marriage forced me to look at life in a completely different way. It broke me down. I had to deal with many shattered pieces which caused me to grow up faster than a lot of my peers.

Not long after my parents' divorce, I became a teen mom. I made the decision to have my child, even though many, many people discouraged me from doing so, but I knew that my baby was mine, that she was a blessing, that she had been given to me by God. Yes, I was young, but I was not done just because of my age. When I was having a difficult time on my journey, all I could think about was the promise God had told me, and I knew that everything was going to fall into place. All I could think about was getting back on my feet, and when I did, I did not stop. All those situations could have been too much for some people, but I refused to be defined by anyone, especially by anyone who wasn't a part of God's plan for my life. Instead, I decided that I was going to take my bad and turn it into good. When I did that, I realized that I had been winning all along, and I hope you know that you are winning, too.

Today, I am happily married to my childhood best friend and the father of my children. I am a published author. I am a life coach. I am a motivational speaker, and I am an entrepreneur. No one saw this for me but God and myself. No one told me, "Hey, Tiffany! You are a winner. You are going to achieve a lot, no matter how long it takes." Instead, I had to go out there and prove to myself that I am not who they have written me off to be, so I want to encourage you to do the same thing.

Winning in this life means having God by your side every step of the way. You don't have to be on social media every second showing off how great your life is. In actuality, I would say you should do the opposite because we all know that, most of the time, what we see on social media is more like a fairy tale. It, often, truly is "Reality Versus Fake Reality," which is one of my favorite chapters in *Born to Change*. Most people go to social media for validation, so I would say, "Live your life. You don't have to put it out there because you know in your heart that you are winning."

Celebrate the beauty of your future. Celebrate that you have a future to look forward to. Each day that you wake up is another chance to win at life. I say, seize that opportunity and make the most of it. You are a child of God, and he only wants the best for you. When he puts a new desire in your heart, he will also give you the tools that are necessary to make that goal a reality, so even when circumstances seem bleak, know that you can change them. Know that you will change them. You already know how to change them. You are winning! And you're going to keep winning because that's what you were put on this earth to do.

***

In *Born to Change*, I encouraged you to become the person God created you to be. Now that you have done that, we are celebrating. Now that you have done that, I want you to think about how awesome you are and how far you've come. You changed! You bettered yourself! And by doing that, you improved your life and made the world a better place. How amazing is that?

If you continue to love yourself and put your trust in God, do you know how unstoppable you will become?

***

As you celebrate winning, I want you to look around and be proud. I truly want you to celebrate all that you have accomplished. It doesn't matter if it took you five seconds, five minutes, five months, five years, or fifty years to change. The important thing is that you did it. You saw that you needed to change, and you changed. It doesn't matter if you just stopped biting your nails or if you stopped using drugs. The actual change doesn't matter. All that matters is how that change affected you.

Do you feel happier? Are you proud of yourself? Do you know that you have just made God so proud of you? I hope you know what changing has done to make your life ten times better than it was before. If you don't, that's why I am here. It's my job to tell you and to remind you that change is you and you are change. Every time you think positive, you win, and every time you win, I want you to celebrate because you deserve it.

Let's take a moment to truly celebrate your win. What are you winning at? What have you accomplished? What are you doing that you are happy about? Take some time and celebrate these changes because they are positive and because they are good for you. Sometimes, we can become so caught up in the negative that we forget to look at all the great things that are happening in our lives. Positivity and changing should always be celebrated, especially if you improved something that you thought was impossible. Be your own motivator. Be proud of yourself. Be happy about the person you have become and are becoming. You are doing great. You are winning.

Be Thankful

"Be thankful that it didn't work out the way you wanted. God's plan is bigger."

~ Tiffany Robinson

I am so thankful to God for all the changes that he has made in my life. Sometimes, when I sit and think about all that God has done for me, all I can do is cry tears of joy. I would never say that I don't deserve all that he has given me in my life, but I will always say that I am awed by his love for me.

As I stated in the previous chapter, it was once very easy for people to write me off because all they did was judge. They didn't see my potential. They didn't see that, despite everything that has happened to me, I know that God has always had a calling on my life. They didn't see that, despite everything that has happened to me, I knew that God was continually blessing me with his grace and mercy. They didn't know how far God was going to bring me. They didn't see how much I relied on him, how much I prayed to him, how obedient I've been. And I am sure the same thing has happened to you. I am sure that people have written you off because all they see is the external. They don't see the internal. They don't see your heart, and it probably isn't meant for them to see what God is seeing right now.

What I know is what God has shown me. What I know is what God has placed on my heart. He has shown me how to be an amazing mom, despite giving birth to my first child at an early age. He has shown me that I can have a family. He has made me the wife of my best friend, and for that, I am eternally grateful. He has given me my own home, even though I was once unsure where I would sleep each night. If he has done all this for me, why wouldn't he do it for you?

If you have gotten this far and haven't changed, it is probably because you have a fear that you might not deserve it. Believe me. I've been there, thinking that I didn't deserve to have a better life because it seemed so impossible to move past my circumstances. I had to start being thankful for what I had, in order to start getting more of what I wanted. I thank God every day for everything. I am thankful for every blessing, big and small, because they all add up to what my life is right now, and I truly wouldn't want it any other way.

I am so thankful that I am able to write these words to you, and I know that God connected me and you, so you could hear this message. I want to encourage you to be thankful. Be thankful for the smallest change. Be thankful for the air you breathe, the water you drink, the sun on your face. Be thankful for these things, and soon, you will be thankful for the big things, the new job, the bills being paid, the clean bill of health, the marriage restored, or the baby that you were told you could never have.

Be thankful and you will always be blessed. Be thankful and you will always be a light for others. Be thankful and every change you make will improve your life.

Stay Humble

"Be original and remain humble."

~ Tiffany Robinson

When I was twenty-five, I started mentoring people. This is what I have been called to do, and my whole life has been preparing me for this. Interestingly, most of the people who sought my guidance were twice my age. The reason they would come to me was because I never judged them. I believed, just because they were older than me and needed some help or advice, that didn't give me the right to look down on them. I learned very early on that we are all on our own journeys, and we all come to different stages and changes at different times. One person might be spiritually mature at ten years old, while someone who has been on this earth for sixty-eight years might not have changed since he or she was fifteen, but God will be there when that person is ready to change, and that is the beautiful thing about this life.

I know that life will humble you. I have learned to be humble in the midst of my journey because I know changing does not make me perfect. Yes, I may have improved certain aspects of my life, but I still have other things to improve, and, yes, we are celebrating those changes in this book, but I want you to always be aware of your humility. God allowed you to change. He placed that desire on your heart and made sure to give you the tools you needed. If you believe that you were the only one responsible for your change, it will be tough to stay humble. Staying and being humble means that you don't judge those harshly who have not changed. As I said earlier, we are all on different paths and at different levels of maturity. Some of us are moving fast, while others are moving a little slower. We must stay humble while we are growing because this helps us to remember that we are works in progress and we are progressing because of the grace of God.

Staying humble keeps me centered and focused. Staying humble also allows setbacks to not be as overwhelming. Know that God will give you what is meant for you at the right time. As a matter of fact, staying humble and being thankful combine perfectly and affect the greatest change.

You're Not Alone

"Faith will lead you. Fear will chase you, and God will forever be with you."

~ Tiffany Robinson

As I stated earlier, many years ago, I became a teen mom, even when everybody around me discouraged me. People told me to do things that didn't align with my heart, but God told me to keep my baby. If I hadn't listened to God and, instead, listened to everybody else, I might not be the person I am today, and I would be living with a regret that somebody else had given to me.

What I am saying is, if you're making a change, you must have faith. You must believe in God because that's who you're going to rely on the whole time. You can't say, "Well, you know what? I'm taking a chance, and I'm investing in myself 'cause my spouse told me to do this or because I spoke to my friend and she encouraged me to go ahead and do this, or I told my mom and she told me to do something else." No, God has to be the one who tells you to do it, not someone else, so guess what? If it doesn't work out, you can't point your finger at your spouse, your friend, or your mother. The only person you can point the finger at is you, because, see, once you live from the inside, you're really living as the person God created you to be. God is the within, and nobody else can see that but you. You can't see my faith, not even if I sat here and told you all about it, not even if you spent a whole day with me. You might not ever understand it. You don't see what I see. It's not for you to see it the way that I see it because I am the one who has to go through the process, not you. You might look at the bigger picture and think, Oh, my God, she's very powerful. She's very loving. She's very kind. She's very spiritual. I can see her future being bright.

But do you see me praying at night? Do you see me being obedient? Do you see me sacrificing? You don't see that, and you haven't seen what I've gone through to get here because that's not the part that I'm sharing. That's the part that I'm working. Like right now, I have another job that I have to go to. I'm sacrificing. That's what I want you to understand. Change is about sacrifice. It's not always easy. Sometimes, it's very hard, but God is with you every step of the way.

***

Even though you might not have someone physically by your side, know that God is with you. You have never been and will never be alone, so please banish that thought from your mind. You know how to change, and by now, you know that you made that decision because you realized God was with you, so why would he place it on your heart to continue growing only to leave you to do it by yourself? You and I both know that that is not a characteristic of the God we serve. Instead, we can count on his leadership and guidance. We know that any and everything we need will come to us right when we need it because he loves us and wants us to succeed in this life.

You are not alone. You never have been, and you never will be. If you ever feel that you are alone, that means it is time to talk to God. Maybe you are feeling a little alone because you haven't prayed or maybe you did something that you know goes against what you are being guided to do. Don't worry. All you have to do is acknowledge this and get back on track. Sometimes, it is easier said than done, but you can do any and everything you put your mind to. I am sure you know that he would never give you a burden that is too great to bear, so you have to know that this journey was created for you. Now that new you is the real you, and any other change will continue to be what is best for you. Knowing this, you should feel some relief. Know that God would never ask a zebra to change its stripes, so he did not create you without a vision. Yes, some learning experiences may be dramatic, but ultimately, they will make your life better. You are being guided and watched over by your creator who has loved you since before you existed. With God on your side, you can never fail, and you're never alone.

You Got This!

"Don't give up. Success is calling your name. Faith is saying, 'I believe you.' God is with you, and your future is waiting on you."

~ Tiffany Robinson

Yes, you got this! At this point, I feel like I shouldn't even have to tell you this. You should just know it. You know all about *life after the change*. You know you *gotta go through it to get to it*. You know you cannot *limit yourself*. You know *your future is calling* and how to *follow the leader*. You know that you are *winning* and that you must *be thankful* and *stay humble*. And in the last chapter, you learned that *you're not alone*. You have so much to celebrate!

Do you realize how smart, strong, and capable you are? You have made changes that have positively impacted your life. You've made these changes because you wanted to improve your life. What could be better than this?

By using the discernment that God has given you, you have put God first and followed his lead. You see the miracles that God gives us every day, and you know that your life is a miracle. How about giving yourself a hand for being able to realize this and using it in a way to make your life better?

My big question is: What is your next plan?

Whether you plan to stop biting your nails or you plan to buy a house…You got this!

Whether you plan to go back to school or get a new job…You got this!

Whether you plan to move across the country or lose twenty pounds...You got this!

Whether you plan to improve your credit or find the love of your life...You got this!

Repeat after me: You got this! You got this! You got this!

Believe me. God did not bring you this far, just to leave you. So know, you got this. You always have, and you always will.

***

I want you to know that my faith was tested early on. My faith has basically been tested at levels I never imagined it could be, but I've learned, the more you change, the harder the fight. I thought I could battle alone. The best example of this was my home-buying process. In the midst of the search for my home, I was ready to give up, but God kept telling me to keep looking. I looked at so many homes that, at one point, they became a blur, but none of them seemed to be what I was looking for. I was at the point where I was ready to say, "You know what, God? I think I need to wait." Before I even said those words out loud, I heard him say, "I've brought you this far, and you've obeyed me at every other turn, but now this is how you're gonna do me?

You're gonna give up?" At that moment, I knew what he had spoken was the truth, and that next week, I found my home. Not only did I find my new home, I, also, won the bid and got equity in it.

So that's how God works, and I'll be honest, after writing and publishing *Born to Change*, I thought I was so on top of everything because of my relationship with God, because of my bond with him and my obedience to him. I thought that anything that came my way would be knocked out the park because of the strength God had blessed me with. I've been asked numerous times, "How do you live such a strong life?" I tell these people, "Without God, I am nothing." They don't know how many times I've gone to God, and how many times he's had to slap me in the face and say, "Hey! You're a leader. You got this."

I don't give up because God lifts me up, and I don't have to reach out to anybody because, when I fall, God picks me up. I've learned that people's words don't really matter. I've often had to tell myself, "Forget what they're saying 'cause they ain't really living it." Do you know what I mean? I'm the one who has to live it, not them, so they don't feel the frustration that I feel, especially just after he had slapped me in my face like that. That was something that tested me. I will ask again, "Do you know what I mean?"

Not long after publishing *Born to Change*, I thought I was all ready to write *Life after the Change*, but God wouldn't allow me to write it because he said, "No, there's still more." This was before I achieved the level I am on now. I soon realized that I couldn't write about something that I hadn't experienced yet. I thought I was ready, but really, I wasn't.

So now I'm actually and really living *life after the change*. I'm really and truly living it now. I have a home. I have my own business. I have more than what I did when I wrote *Born to Change*. And it's all because of *life after the change*. It's all because I made the decision to stick with God. After all of this, so much more has come, but I have always had a vision.

See, one thing about my life's journey is that, when I was a little girl, I would stand in front of the fire place, talking to my doll babies as if they were an audience of real people. My family thought I was crazy, but now that I am living in my vision, I know it was all a part of God's plan. My family will tell you that I have always been different, but now it makes more sense when I look back. It must have been kinda hard for them, trying to understand me. As I stood up, acting as if I was encouraging and uplifting my audience in my head (LOL!), they would always ask, "Girl, who are you talkin' to?" They would also ask, "Where are the people?"

What they didn't know was that, from an early age, I had a vision. I still have a vision, and, along the way to reaching my provision, I still have to *go through it to get to it*.

***

So, hey, congratulations! You did it, and when I say, "You did it!" I mean, you *really* did it, whether what you did was a big 180 or something that seems insignificant; nonetheless, you've changed, but remember, you're still changing, and you're always gonna be changing, so don't think that this is it for you. You're gonna continue to battle as you grow, but this is because you'll always need to make necessary improvements while on your journey.

One thing I know for sure is that there's nothing I can do but continue to listen to and follow God. I am here to tell you that you're going to continue to change. A lot of people are afraid to change one thing about themselves because they don't want to change again and again. They know that, after that one change, a domino effect might ensue. Thank God that you weren't afraid because so many people say, "I want to own my own business and be an entrepreneur, but I am afraid to leave my job. Owning my own business might force me to do or learn something different, or it might force me to move to a different city, move from the house that I'm in, and get me out of the comfort zone I'm in."

Think about people who are afraid to buy a home. They're so comfortable with paying rent, and they don't think they can buy a home because it might come with a few extra bills, so they talk themselves out of it. I just want you to know that, no matter what, change is never going to leave us because it's a part of us. It's okay to change, as I've already said. Changing shows that you love yourself. You have to be coming from a place of love and not from a place of fear, and you have to know that God is with you every step of the way.

***

Please understand that, just because you have changed, doesn't mean you're still the same. You might have changed one thing, like stealing, but you might still be lying. Changing doesn't make you perfect. You've only fixed one thing, but you still have other things to work on. We all do.

Just because you've lost the weight doesn't mean you're not going to be tempted by chocolate cakes and gallons of ice cream. You know you're always going to be fighting your own battle. You're going to have to be tough.

For example, just because you stopped doing drugs today doesn't mean you should hurry to the trap house the next day because you might not be strong enough to do that. Eventually, you are going to have to be tempted. You are going to have to return to your old stomping grounds and fight that urge, but not today. You have to be gentle with yourself. When you are no longer tempted, then you can say, "Man, hey, I'm a changed person. I don't do that no more!" But you don't want to test it before you're ready because that's how you might fail, and you don't want to go backward when you've come so far.

No one would say the day after they've kicked a drug habit, "I've been clean for twenty-four hours, so let me go hang out with my drug-dealing, drug-taking friends." But I want you to know that God is really real, and he's going to help you no matter what type of situation you are in and no matter what it is. If it's weight loss, drug dealing, drug abuse, relationship problems…no matter what it is, God will order your steps. At the end of the day, God is giving you an abundance of love and an abundance of the ability to flourish.

***

Let me tell you, I live from the bottom up, and the reason I say this is because these are my three cores: I live from my heart. I speak it. I tell my mind; instead of my mind telling me, I tell my mind because our minds can tell us to do some terrible things, but if I allow my heart to tell my mouth to my mind, then I am going somewhere, and I remain humble versus my mind telling me to not listen to my heart.

***

You've got this because God wants you to have this. You know how to change. You know how to work hard, and you know that you can and will do anything you set your heart and mind to. Change is a beautiful thing because it is a constant in our lives. We would be cheating ourselves if we did not change. It is a part of our lives, and it is inevitable, but we know we can also change what we need to in order to continue improving our lives. If God has put a desire in your heart, know that you got this. If God has spoken to you, know that you got this. I am not worried. I know that you can and will achieve any and everything you want. You got this!

121

About the Author

Tiffany Robinson is a Hampton, Virginia native currently residing in Atlanta, Georgia, with her loving husband and two amazing daughters.

Tiffany credits being raised in a two-parent home where there was an abundance of love and attention as her foundation. Her childhood was picture perfect...until the day her parents announced they were getting a divorce.

Unexpectedly, her perfect world was turned upside down and filled with turmoil and angst. Tiffany suffered from depression, faced unimaginable challenges, and unexpected changes throughout her teenage years. She often asked herself, "Why me?"

Looking back, Tiffany understands all the heartache and pain she endured was a necessary journey for her to learn compassion and humility, and to strengthen her relationship with God.

Today, Tiffany Robinson fully devotes herself to helping others who are in need of guidance, resolve, enlightenment, and a sense of purpose. It's her passion to help her clients find their breakthrough to a better life and to see their dreams become a reality.

Not only does it give her a sense of purpose, Tiffany finds the experience of helping others incredibly rewarding.

If you would like to schedule a life coaching session or a speaking engagement, please visit Tiffany's website at

www.TiffanyTooReal.com. Please feel free to follow her on

Twitter and Instagram: @TiffanyTooReal

Please like her Facebook page: @TiffanyTooReal

Subscribe to her YouTube channel: TiffanyTooReal

www.ingramcontent.com/pod-product-compliance
Lightning Source LLC
Chambersburg PA
CBHW060159100426
42744CB00007B/1092